WILDFLOWERS

OF THE LITTLE TENNESSEE RIVER GREENWAY

FRIENDS OF

THE GREENWAY

FRANKLIN, NORTH CAROLINA

© FRIENDS OF THE GREENWAY, INC
573 E. Main St.
Franklin, North Carolina
(828) 369-8488

LittleTennessee.org

ISBN 978-1-7374003-4-9

Plant Identification . . . FROGs Eyes

Editing . . . Kay Coriell, Sally Kesler

Photography . . . Ellen Bishop, Hollis Walker,
Mary Browning & Rita St. Clair

Interior Design & Map . . . Hank Shuler

Cover Design . . . Monica Collier

Forward

The lives of many people are richer because of a feisty lady named Sally Kesler. Diminutive in body and gargantuan in spirit, she breathes fire when "her plants" are threatened. It is to this wonderful lady, Sally the Magic Dragon, that this book is dedicated.

The founder of the Friends of the Greenway and the FROGs Eyes, Miss Sally can be spotted purposefully, never leisurely, walking the Greenway, checking out all her children - the flora and fauna of the Little Tennessee River Greenway.

Under her tutelage, the FROGs Eyes have cataloged over 300 species of plants on the Greenway. This book containing 75 wild flowers and the seed pods or fruit of 14 wild flowers, trees, and shrubs' represents about 20% of those cataloged.

A dedicated group of people, the FROGs Eyes, mark blooming flowers of interest, in addition to cataloging and generally "guarding" them.

It is our hope that you will use this book to enhance your pleasure of the Greenway. Use it to record when and where you sight these wonderful treasures. But please, don't pick the daisies, or any other wild flowers for that matter.

The various flowers in this guide are grouped by color. The common and scientific names used are found in *Newcomb's Wildflower Guide* and *Vascular Flora of the Carolinas*.

Specified locations are trail sections where the plant has been spotted by the FROGs Eyes.

Little Tennessee River
GREENWAY

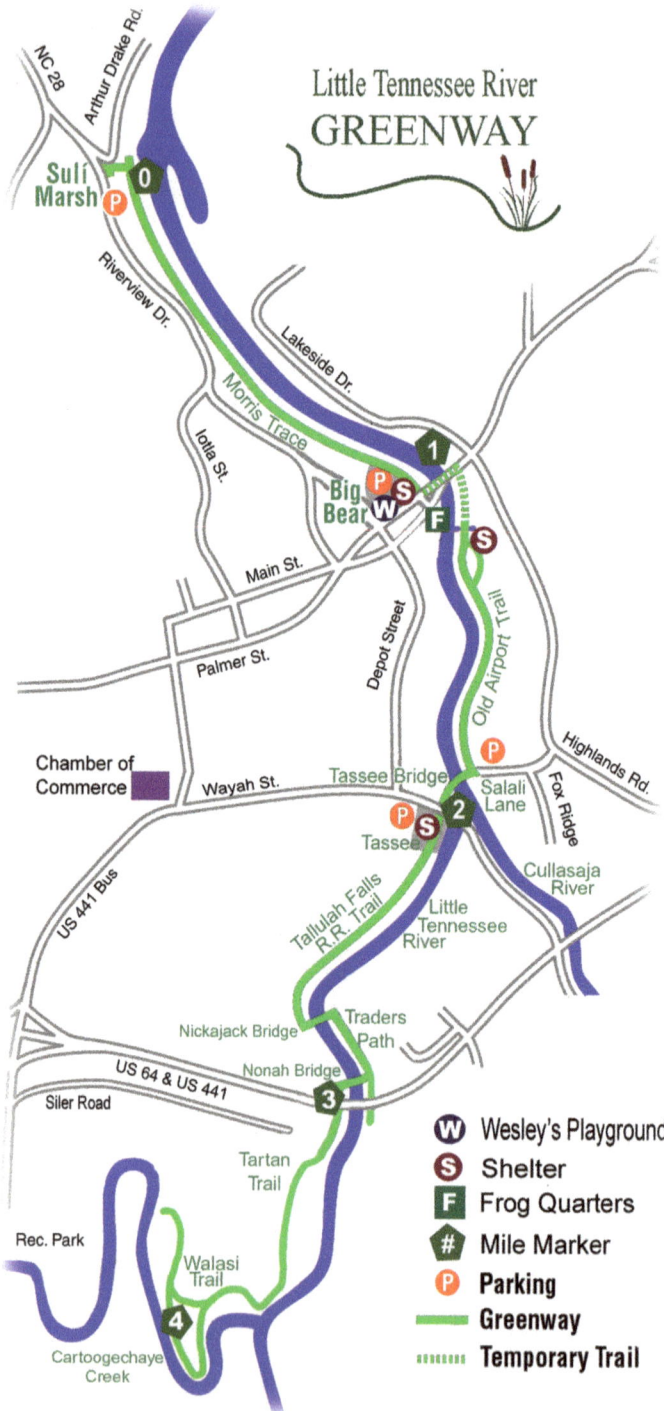

NC 28

Arthur Drake Rd.

Sulí Marsh Ⓟ ⓪

Riverview Dr.

Lakeside Dr.

Morris Trace

Iotla St.

Big Bear Ⓟ Ⓢ Ⓦ ① Ⓕ Ⓢ

Main St.

Palmer St.

Depot Street

Old Airport Trail

Highlands Rd.

Chamber of Commerce

Wayah St.

Tassee Bridge

Ⓟ

Salali Lane

Fox Ridge

Ⓟ Ⓢ ② **Tassee**

Cullasaja River

US 441 Bus

Tallulah Falls R.R. Trail

Little Tennessee River

Nickajack Bridge

Traders Path

US 64 & US 441

Nonah Bridge

Siler Road

③

Tartan Trail

Rec. Park

Walasi Trail

④

Cartoogechaye Creek

Ⓦ **Wesley's Playground**
Ⓢ **Shelter**
Ⓕ **Frog Quarters**
Mile Marker
Ⓟ **Parking**
— **Greenway**
······· **Temporary Trail**

Contents

Contents

Pink Flowers

Lavender Flowers

Purple Flowers

Blue Flowers

Fruit & Seeds

Oxeye Daisy
Chrysanthemum leucanthemum

With its golden center ringed with white petals, the common daisy lights up any landscape. It blooms spring through fall.

1 to 3' high plant with dark green coarsely toothed leaves with a flower head of 1 to 2".

Composite family

Morris Trace, Tallulah Falls RR Trail, Tartan Trail

_____

_____

_____

_____

_____

_____

Daisy Fleabane
Erigeron annuus

Small white daisy-like flowers form an airy cluster over a branching plant in spring and summer. The fleabane name is derived from a belief that the dried flowers could rid a house of fleas.

1 to 5' tall plant, hairy lanceolate leaves, ½" flower heads.

Composite family

All trail sections

White Woodland Aster
Aster divaricatus

White daisy-like flowers atop a zigzag stalk with heart-shaped basal leaves. Blooms late summer into early fall.

1 to 3 ½' tall plant with heart-shaped leaves, 1" flowers.

Composite family

Tallulah Falls RR Trail

_____

_____

_____

_____

_____

_____

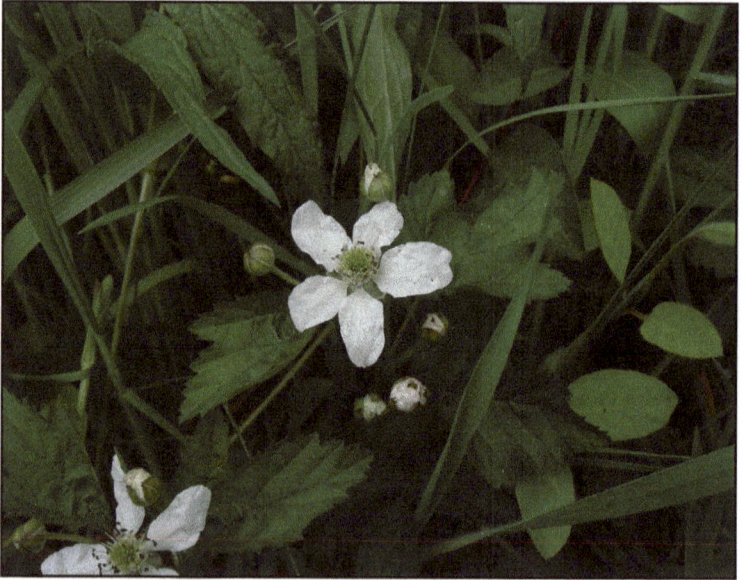

Dewberry
Rubus flagellaris

This trailing vine with prickly stems and leaves, and three to five leaflets, has clear white, five-petalled blooms which produce an edible berry. Look for bloom in spring.

4 to 12" tall plant, ¾" flower.

Rose family

Morris Trace, Tallulah Falls RR Trail

Buttonweed
Diodia teres

Small white flowers like four-pointed stars bloom on these creeping plants during summer and fall.

Creeper with ¼" flowers.

Madder family

Morris Trace, Old Airport Trail, Tallulah Falls RR Trail

Starry Campion
Silene stellata

Petals of these summer bloomers are deeply fringed and leaves grow in whorls of four. They prefer rich woodlands.

2 to 3' tall plant, long leaves clustered in whorls of 4, ¾" flowers.

Pink family

Tallulah Falls RR Trail, Walasi Trail

Virgin's Bower Clematis
Clematis virginiana

Three leaved vine displays masses of white flowers. The feathery seed clusters remain during much of the winter. The seed clusters (inset) of this lovely vine mimic a fleecy flower.

6 to 10 vine stems, 1" flowers with 4 petallike sepals.

Buttercup family

All trail sections

Boneset
Eupatorium perfoliatum

Growing in damp ground, the pointed leaves of this plant clasp the stem. Boneset tea is brewed from the dried leaves of this fall bloomer.

2 to 5' tall, each flower in the cluster is less than ¼" on this hairy plant that enjoys low woods and wet meadows.

Composite family

Morris Trace

_____

_____

_____

_____

_____

_____

Water Hemlock
Cicuta maculata

Lacy white umbels bloom in summer atop tall stalks. All parts of the plant, which grows in Sulí Marsh, are poisonous to humans and livestock alike.

3 to 6' tall, each flower is the cluster is less than ¼", very pretty but leave alone.

Parsley family

Morris Trace

_____

_____

_____

_____

_____

_____

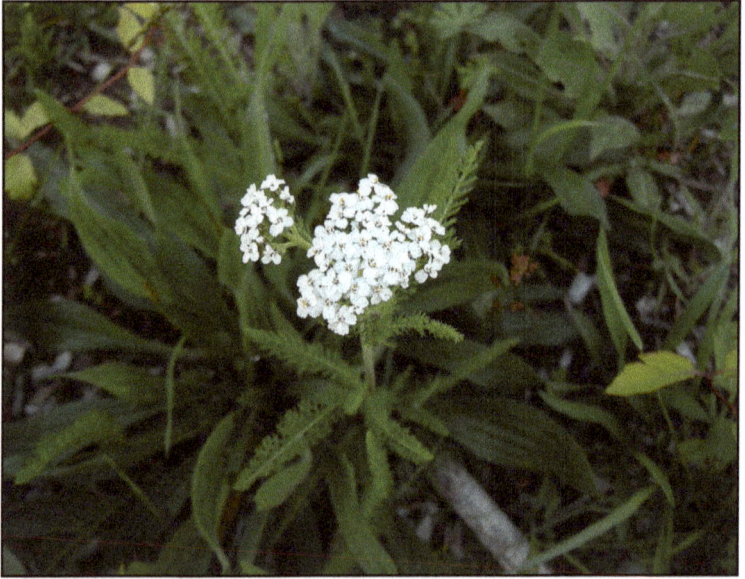

Yarrow
Achillea millefolium

Tiny white flowers form a terminal cluster atop this plant with its fernlike leaves that were steeped by Native Americans to cure stomach problems. Look for blooms in the summer through fall.

1 to 3' tall with clusters of ¼" flowers and gray-green fernlike leaves and hairy stems.

Composite family

Morris Trace, Old Airport Trail.

Queen Anne's Lace
Daucus carota

The round flat cluster of tiny white flowers of this ancestor to the garden carrot attracts many insects: flies, bees, butterflies, wasps, and beetles. Often the central flower of this European native is dark purple or red.

1 to 3' tall with compound umbel of 3 to 5" across and 2 to 8" carrot leaves.

Parsley family

All trail sections

Virginia Spirea
Spirea virginiana

Displaying a flat-topped cluster of white flowers in summer, this rare shrub is quite at home on the Greenway. The plant enjoys growing in meadows, old fields, low moist areas, and on river banks.

2 to 5' tall woody shrub, each flower in the cluster is ¼".

Rose family

Old Airport Trail

Hoary Mountain Mint
Pycnanthemum incanum

This charming member of the mint family has small white to lavender flowers densely clustered in leaf axils. The overall appearance of the plant, which blooms June through September, is a dusty white-green and it has hairy square stems.

1 to 3' tall with ½' flowers, lanceolate-ovate leaves are white beneath.

Mint family

Old Airport Trail, Tallulah Falls RR Trail, Tartan Trail, Walasi Trail

_____

_____

_____

_____

Wild Stonecrop
Sedum ternatum

A creeping plant with rounded leaves in whorls of three and starlike white blooms in April. It is named for its ease in regenerating from almost any fragment. The family includes the Jade Tree and the Kalanchoe.

3 to 6"" tall with ½" flowers and fleshy stems and leaves.

Stonecrop family

Traders Path, Tartan Trail

_____

_____

_____

_____

_____

Dog Hobble
Leucothoe axillaris

Evergreen lance-shaped leaves grow thickly on this arching shrub. Drooping racemes of bell-like flowers appear in spring.

1 to 3' tall with ¾" flowers with woody stalks.

Heath family

Tallulah Falls RR Trail

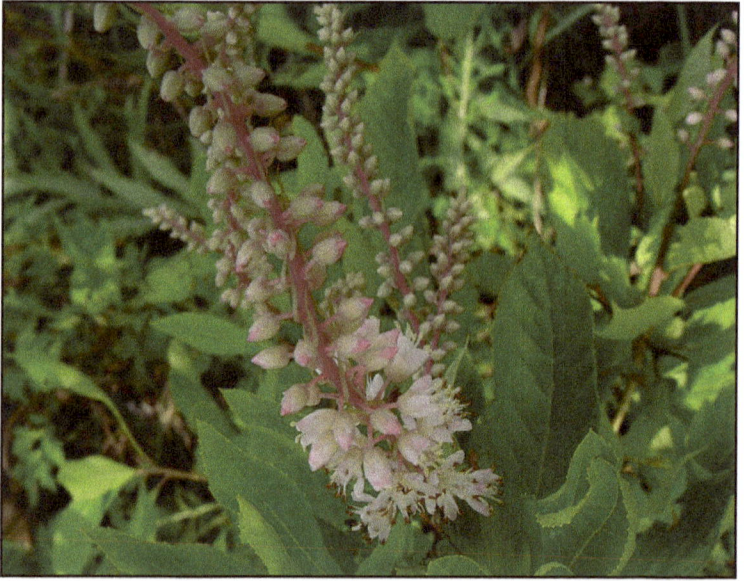

Clethra or Sweet Pepperbush
Clethra acuminata

A shrub with long racemes of pinkish-white flowers. Highly fragrant during summer bloom and very attractive to butterflies.

3 to 10' tall with 3/8" flowers and 3" sharply toothed leaves.

White Alder family

Morris Trace, Old Airport Trail, Tallulah Falls RR Trail

_____

_____

_____

_____

_____

_____

Witch Alder
Fothergilla major

Brush-like fragrant flowers adorn this small shrub in spring. Leaves in fall turn red, orange and gold.

Witch Hazel family

Airport Trail at Salali Lane

Silky Dogwood
Cornus amomum

Broad clusters of small white flowers bloom in the summer on this opposite-leaved small tree which likes moist locations. Look for slightly hairy red twigs and blue fruit in winter.

3 to 15' tall with ¾" flowers.

Dogwood family

Morris Trace, Old Airport Trail, Tallulah Falls RR Trail, Traders Path

_____

_____

_____

_____

_____

_____

Smooth Solomon's Seal
Polygonatum biflorum

Pale-green to whitish trumpet-shaped flowers hang below the leaf axils on a graceful arching stalk. Early settlers and Native Americans used the rhizome for food.

8 to 15" tall with ¾" flowers and 2 to 6" long lanceolate, smooth leaves with distinctly parallel veins.

Lily family

Airport Trail, Tallulah Falls RR Trail, Tartan Trail

_____

_____

_____

_____

Japanese Honeysuckle
Lonicera japonica

This highly fragrant vine that climbs and trails has white flowers that yellow with age. Introduced from Asia, it is a fast grower that can engulf other plants and is hard to eradicate.

30' long vines with 1½" flowers and long, opposite, ovate, untoothed leaves up to 3" long.

Honeysuckle family

All trail sections

Silverbell
Halesia carolina

In April and May the branches of this tree are hung with white bell-shaped blooms. See seed pod on page 88.

30' tall with ½ to 1" flowers and 3 to 6" long pointed leaves. Bark on young trees is striped, mature trees have reddish-brown, scaly bark.

Storax family

All trail sections

Downy Sunflower
Helianthus mollis

This unique plant has opposite grayish-green leaves that clasp the stalk. The clear yellow flowers appear in late summer.

2 to 3' tall with 2" flower.

Composite family

Morris Trace, Old Airport Trail

_____

_____

_____

_____

_____

_____

_____

Tickseed Sunflower
Bidens aristosa

One of the annual wildflowers planted along North Carolina roadsides, this annual produces a shower of golden blooms in September.

1 to 5' tall with 1 to 2" flowers, lobed and toothed leaves up to 6". Can be found in roadside ditches, wet meadows, low ground, and abandoned fields.

Composite family

Morris Trace, Old Airport Trail, Tallulah Falls RR Trail

_____

_____

_____

_____

_____

Jerusalem Artichoke
Helianthus tuberosus

This lovely plant is covered in yellow blooms in late summer and early fall. It was a food source to Native Americans who dug the tuberous root and roasted or boiled them like potatoes. Raw, they have a nutlike taste.

5 to 10' tall with 3" flowers and thick, rough, coarsely-toothed, 6 to 8" long leaves.

Composite family

All trail sections

_____

_____

_____

_____

_____

Mouse-Eared Coreopsis
Coreopsis auriculata

With eight to ten toothed petals, this bright yellow flower blooms around the Greenway picnic shelters and bridges during the summer.

1 to 2' tall with conspicuously toothed 2" flower, most leaves basal.

Composite family

Morris Trace, Airport Trail, Tallulah Falls RR Trail, Tartan Trail

_____

_____

_____

_____

_____

_____

Coreopsis
Coreopsis tinctoria

Heads of toothed yellow rays with red centers bloom abundantly on these branching plants in late spring.

2 to 4' tall with 1 ¼" flowers and 2 to 4" long opposite, highly dissected leaves.

Composite family

Morris Trace, Tallulah Fall RR Trail

_____

_____

_____

_____

_____

_____

Greenheaded Coneflower
Rudbeckia laciniata

This tall plant has deeply cut leaves. Look for the greenish flower heads with drooping yellow rays in summer through fall. Called "Sochan" by the Cherokees, it was a favorite for spring salads.

3 to 6' tall with 2 to 3" flowers, 2 to 7" long leaves.

Composite family

Morris Trace, Old Airport Trail, Tallulah Falls RR Trail, Tartan Trail

Sneezweed
Helenium autumnale

Growing in moist soils, this early fall bloomer has a large domed center surrounded by drooping yellow petals. Stems appear winged. It was believed that the snuff made from its dried leaves would cause sneezing and the ridding of evil spirits.

2 to 5 ' tall with 1 to 2" flowers and leaves up to 6" long with bases forming winged extensions down the stem.

Composite family

Morris Trace, Tallulah Falls RR Trail

_____

_____

_____

_____

Black-Eyed Susan
Rudbeckia hirta

Atop a rough hairy stem, the yellow petals of this biennial summer and fall bloomer frame a dark domed center.

1 to 3' tall with 2 to 3" flowers, 2 to 7" leaves that are rough, hairy and lanceolate to ovate.

Composite family

Morris Trace, Tallulah Falls RR Trail, Traders Path

_____

_____

_____

_____

_____

Bulbous Buttercup
Ranunculus bulbosus

Five shining, golden-yellow petals typify the spring blooming buttercups. Leaves are usually three-parted. Plant is somewhat poisonous and will affect cattle if eaten fresh but it has no effect when dried and eaten as hay.

1 to 2' tall with 1" flowers, it is a hairy plant with a bulbous base.

Buttercup family

All trail sections

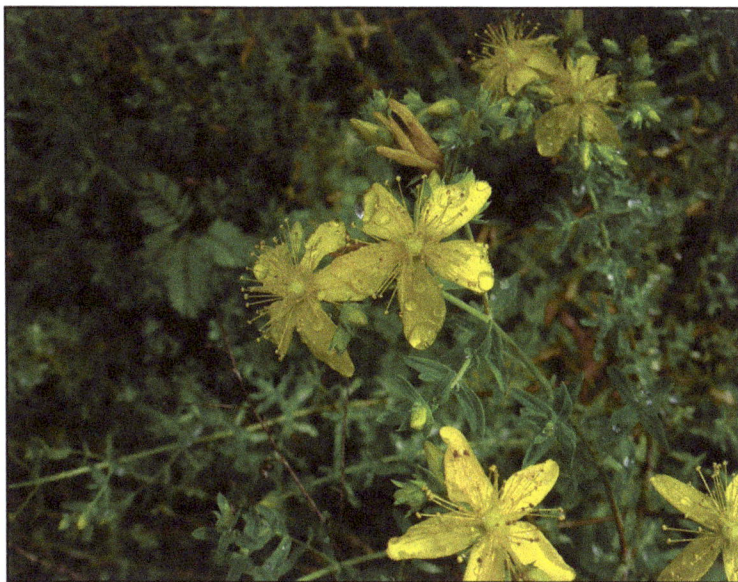

St. John's Wort
Hypericum perforatum

An erect herb with opposite leaves and numerous branching clusters of five-petaled yellow flowers said to bloom on St. John's Eve - June 24. Introduced from Europe, causes increased sensitivity to sunlight if taken medicinally.

1 to 2½' tall with ¾ to 1" flowers and 1 to 2" leaves.

St. John's Wort family

Morris Trace, Old Airport Trail, Tallulah Falls RR Trail, Tartan Trail

_____

_____

_____

_____

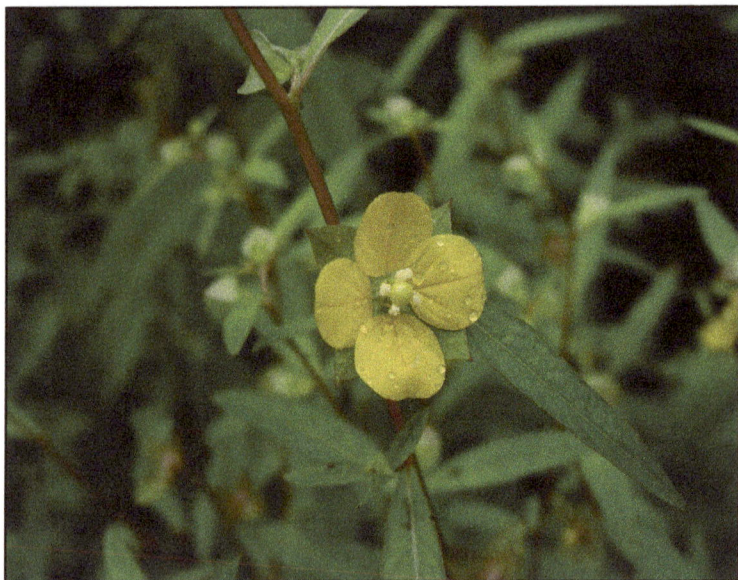

Seedbox
Ludwigia alternifolia

This summer bloomer is a four-petalled yellow flower growing in leaf axils that produce boxlike seed capsules in the fall. See page 89 for the seed pods.

2 to 3' tall with ½" flowers and 2 to 4" long lanceolate, untoothed leaves.

Evening Primrose family

Morris Trace, Old Airport Trail, Tallulah Falls RR Trail

_____

_____

_____

_____

_____

_____

Fringed Loosestrife
Lysimachia ciliata

An erect planting having opposite leaves with fringed stems. The five yellow petals are toothed at the tip of this summer bloomer.

1 to 4' tall with ¾" minutely toothed flowers and 2½ to 5" leaves.

Primrose family

Tallulah Falls RR Trail

_____

_____

_____

_____

_____

_____

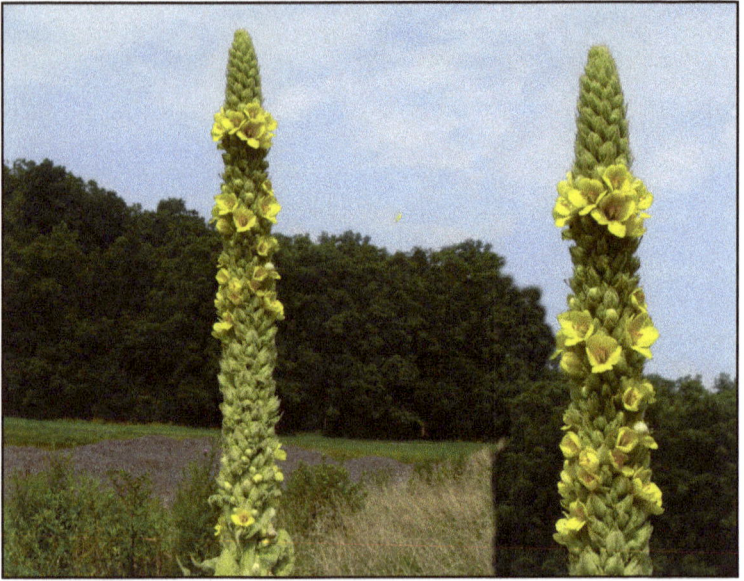

Common Mullein
Verbascum thapsus

A tall woolly plant with a long spike of lemon-yellow flowers in the summer. Roman soldiers used its flower spikes for torches. Naive Americans lined their moccasins with its leaves. Naturalized from Europe, its leaves have been brewed into a tea to treat everything from earaches to the croup.

2 to 7' tall with ¾" flowers and 1' long leaves continuing down the stem as thin ridges.

Figwort family

All trail sections

_____

_____

_____

_____

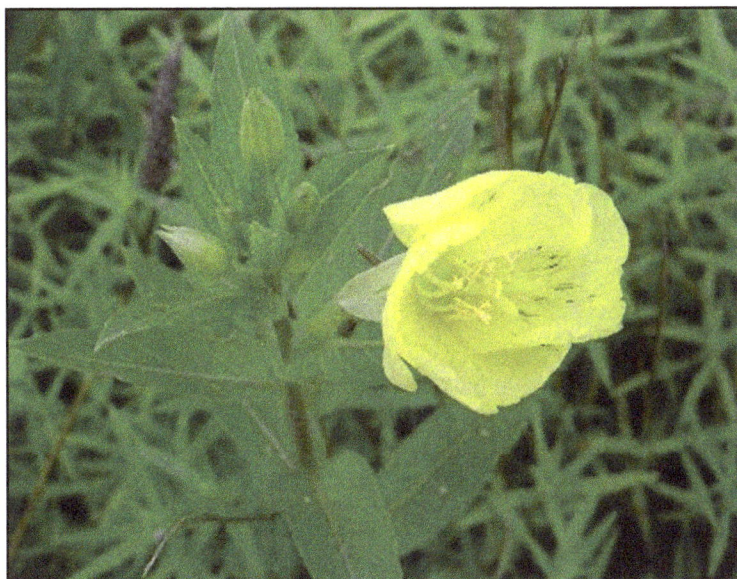

Evening Primrose
Oenothera biennis

On a robust plant, four-petalled canary yellow flowers unroll pointed buds from midsummer until frost. The flowers of this biennial open near sundown and generally close by noon.

2 to 5' tall with 1 to 2" flowers and 4 to 8" slightly toothed, lanceolate leaves.

Evening Primrose family

All trail sections

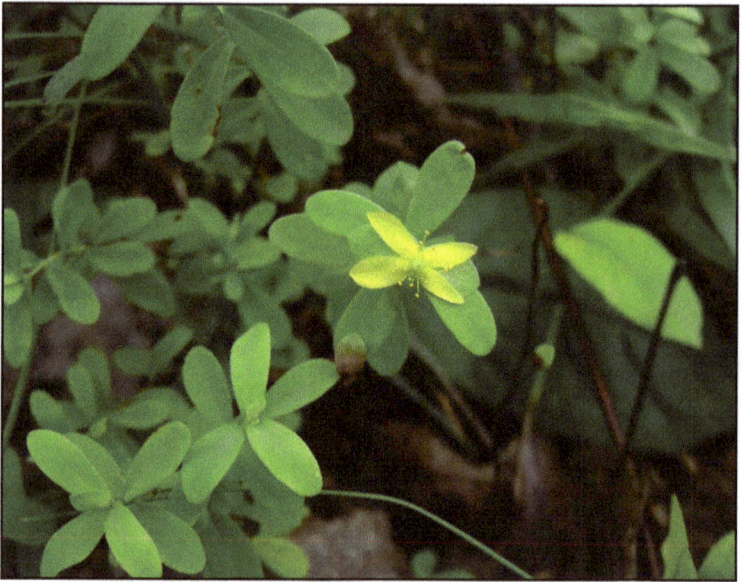

St. Andrew's Cross
Hypericum hypericoides

This diminutive bloomer likes sandy soils and can be recognized by its four-petaled yellow flower above a cluster of four leaves. The name is derived from its clusters of four leaves and petals.

2½ to 6" tall with ½" flowers and 1" narrow leaves.

St. John's Wort family

Morris Trace, Old Airport Trail, Tallulah Falls RR Trail

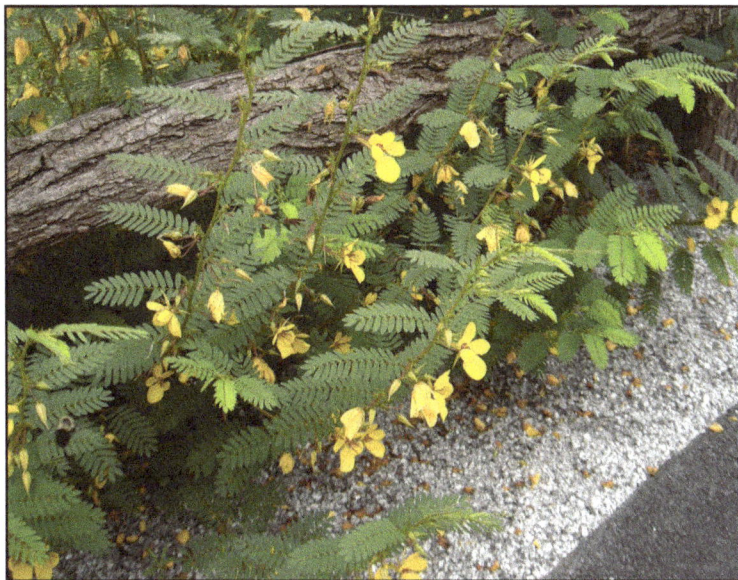

Partridge Pea
Cassia fasciculata

The eight to 15 pairs of pinnate leaves of this erect plant surround the showy five-petalled yellow flowers found blooming in summer and fall.

6 to 30" tall with 1 to 1½" flowers.

Pea family

Morris Trace, Old Airport Trail, Tallulah Falls RR Trail, Traders Path

_____

_____

_____

_____

_____

_____

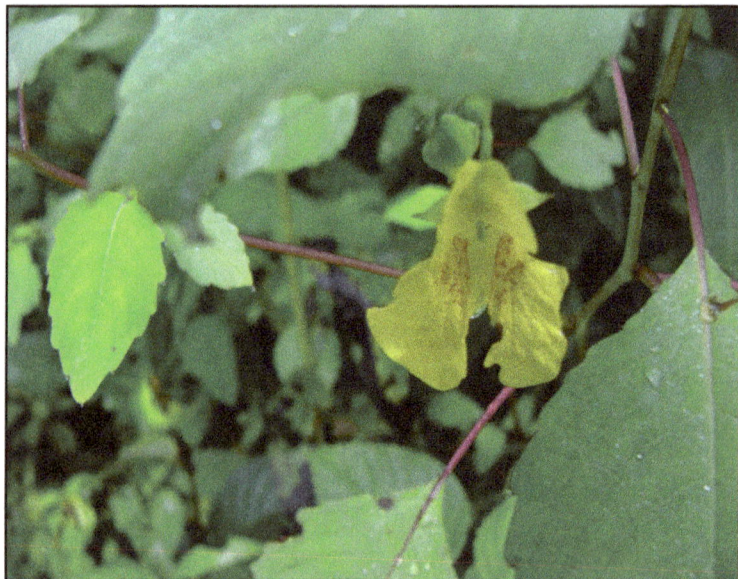

Pale Jewel Weed or Touch-Me-Not
Impatiens pallida

Often found at higher altitudes, this summer to early fall-blooming yellow jewelweed has several colonies on the Greenway. The soft-stemmed cousin of the Spotted Touch-Me-Not is less common.

3 to 6' tall with 1½" flowers and 1 to 4" long, alternate, ovate, thin leaves.

Touch-Me-Not family

Old Airport Trail, Traders Path

_____

_____

_____

_____

_____

_____

Lance-Leaved Goldenrod
Solidago graminifolia

Flat-topped clusters of tiny flowers grow on this erect branching plant. This late summer and fall bloomer is happy growing along roadsides, fields, and thickets.

2 to 4' tall with tiny ¼" flowers clustered along the end of the stalks and ¼" wide leaves.

Composite family

Tallulah Falls RR Trail

Butterfly Weed
Asclepias tuberosa

Clusters of bright orange flowers in the summer attract butterflies and human eyes to the only milkweed without a milky sap. Its tough root was chewed by Native Americans to cure pleurisy.

1 to 2½' tall with 3/8" flowers in clusters and 2 to 6" long oblong, narrow leaves.

Milkweed family

Tallulah Falls RR Trail

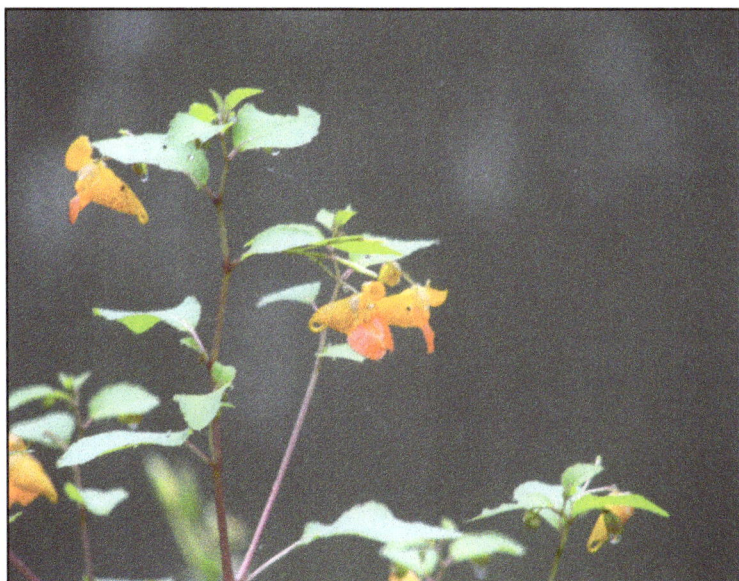

Orange Jewel Weed or
Spotted Touch-Me-Not
Impatiens capensis

Orange flowers dangle from a long stalk in summer and early fall. Mature seed pods burst suddenly when touched. The sap of this annual's stems and leaves used to relieve poison ivy, nettles, and athlete's foot. Butterflies, bees, and hummingbirds enjoy it. Found in shaded wetlands and woods.

2 to 5' tall with 1" flowers with succulent translucent stems and long, thin, alternate 1½ to 3½" leaves.

Touch-Me-Not family

All trail sections

Cardinal Flower
Lobelia cardinalis

Blazing in moist locations, cardinal flower proclaims RED, with twenty to thirty tubular florets topping a sturdy stalk in the summer. Butterflies are the chief pollinators of this beauty.

2 to 4' tall with ½" flowers and 6" long lanceolate toothed leaves.

Lobelia family

Morris Trace, Old Airport Trail, Tallulah Falls RR Trail

Fire Pink
Silene virginica

On sticky stems with opposite leaves, this star-shaped flower is not pink but bright crimson. Look for the summer blooms.

6 to 24" tall with 1½" flowers and 1½ to 4" long lanceolate basal leaves and 6" long opposite leaves on stalk.

Pink family

Tallulah Falls RR Trail

Sweet Shrub or Sweet Betsy
Calycanthus floridus

The maroon blooms of this opposite-leaved shrub are fragrant with a slightly cinnamon smell during the summer.

3 to 6' tall with 1" blooms.

Sweet Shrub family

Tallulah Falls RR Trail

_____

_____

_____

_____

_____

_____

Gaura
Gaura biennis

Numerous four-petalled flowers with drooping stamens resemble a cloud of butterflies in summer on this branching biennial plant.

2 to 5' tall with 1/3" wide flowers and lance shaped lightly toothed leaves.

Evening Primrose family

Morris Trace, Old Airport Trail, Tallulah Falls RR Trail, Tartan Trail

_____

_____

_____

_____

_____

_____

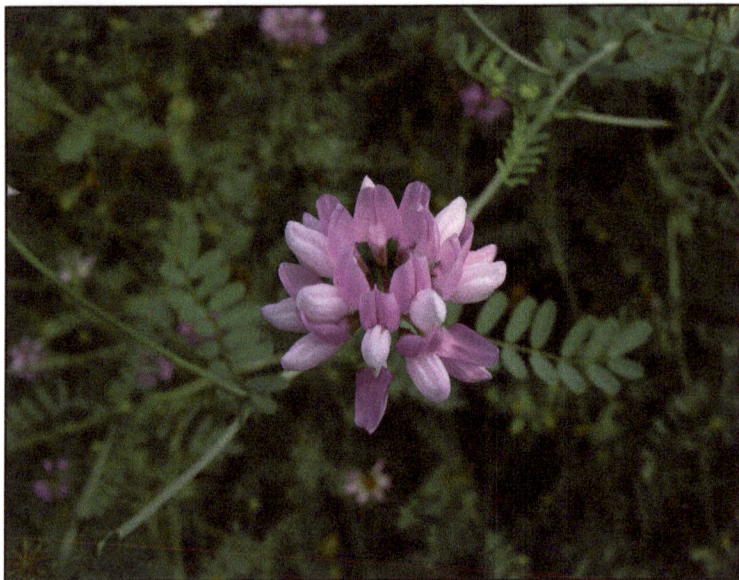

Crown Vetch
Coronilla varia

Pink and white clover-like flowers rise over the dense divided leaves of this aggressive vine in the summer. A European introduction used to stabilize banks.

1 to 2' tall with 1" flowers and 2 to 4" long leaves.

Pea family

Tallulah Fall RR Trail, Traders Path

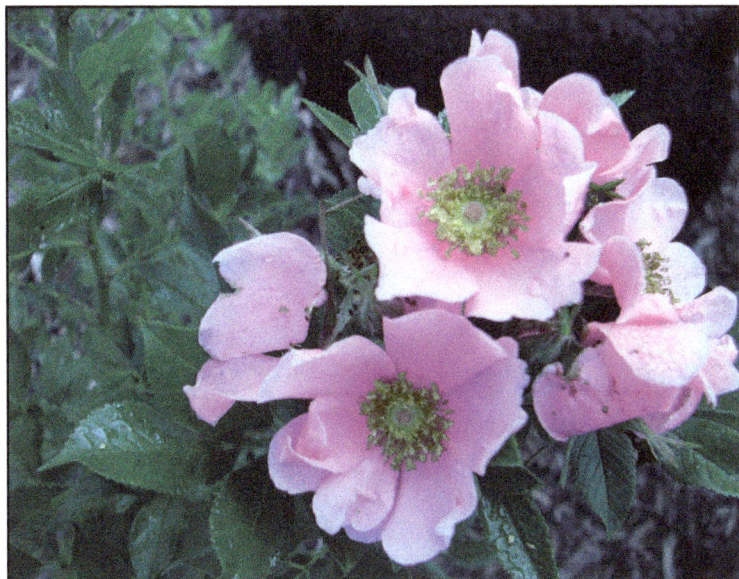

Carolina Rose or Pasture Rose
Rosa carolina

This prickly shrub has single blooms of five pink petals surrounding a golden center in the summer. The fruits are bright red and the upper thorns are straight.

1 to 3' tall with 2" flowers with heavily toothed ovate leaves.

Rose family

Morris Trace, Tallulah Falls RR Trail, Traders Path

_____

_____

_____

_____

_____

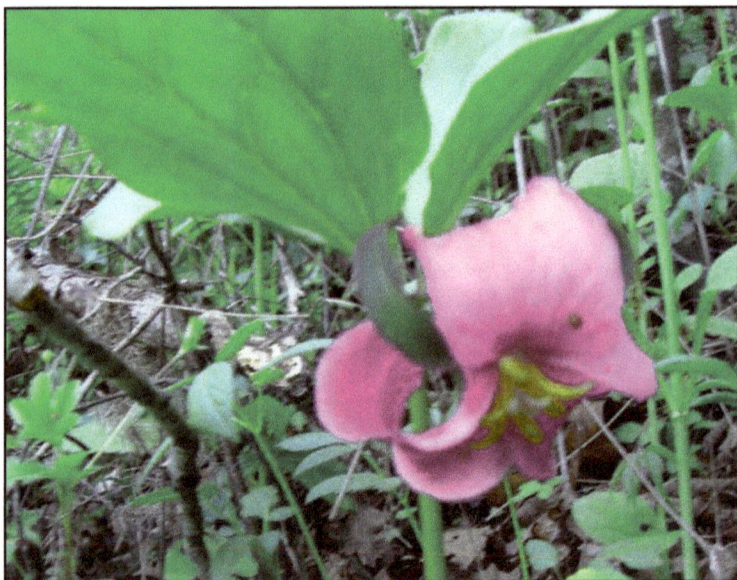

Catesby's Trillium
Trillium catesbaei

With its golden center ringed with pale pink or white petals, the Catesby's Trillium is a three-petalled flower nestled below three leaves, atop a nodding stalk. It prefers a shady woodland setting.

8 to 20" tall with 2 to 3" flower with 3 sepals and 6 stamens.

Lily family

Tallulah Falls RR Trail, Tartan Trail, Walasi Trail

_____

_____

_____

_____

_____

_____

Smartweed
Polygonum sp.

Several species of Smartweed bloom from summer till frost on the Greenway. The showiest, in Suli Marsh, has slender spikes of brightest pink.

1 to 3' tall with 1/8" flowers with 3" long, elliptical leaves.

Buckwheat family

All trail sections

Deptford Pink
Dianthus armeria

The deep pink flowers grow atop a slender erect stem. The five petals have jagged edges and tiny white spots. You may find them blooming between May and September. They are named for a section of London where they grew in profusion.

6 to 15" tall with ½" flowers and a 1 to 4" long, narrow, erect, light green leaf.

Pink family

All trail sections

Summer Phlox
Phlox paniculata

Five rounded petals joined to a slender tube identify a member of the Phlox family. Pink panicles of this tall plant illumine the summer greenery. It has been widely used as a medicinal herb as a laxative and for the treatment of boils.

2 to 6' tall with 1" flowers in clusters with 3 to 5" long opposite, ovate-lanceolate leaves.

Phlox family

All trail sections

Hedge Nettle
Stachys latidens

The square stem of a mint, opposite toothed leaves, and a spike of pink flowers opening from the bottom to the top identify this summer bloomer.

10 to 25" tall with ¾" flowers with deeply toothed hairy leaves.

Mint family

Morris Trace, Old Airport Trail

_____

_____

_____

_____

_____

_____

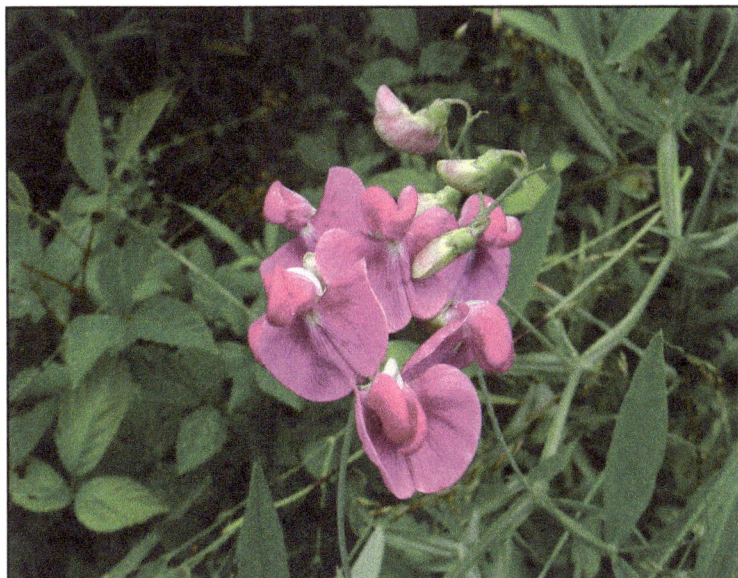

Perennial Pea
Lathyrus latifolius

This vine clambers over its neighbors to lift long racemes of pink flowers and blossoms through the summer.

Vine with ¾" flowers, jointed stems and long ovate leaves.

Pea family

Morris Trace

_____

_____

_____

_____

_____

_____

Purple Gerardia
Gerardia pupurea

Not purple, but pink, this charming funnel-shaped flower with five rounded petals grows in moist places and blooms in the fall.

10 to 14" tall with 1" flower and 1 to 1½" long, thin leaves.

Figwort family

Morris Trace, Tallulah Falls RR Trail

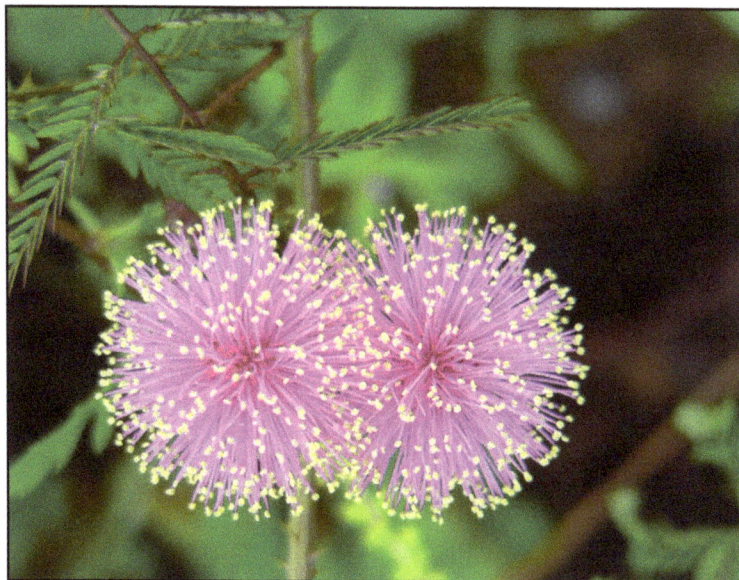

Sensitive Brier
Schrankia microphylla

The many leaflets of this prickly sprawling vine close at a touch. Each round pink head consists of many tiny flowers. Look for summer blooms.

6" vine with ¾" flower cluster and ¼" long leaflets with a vein running on one edge of leaflet.

Pea family

Morris Trace, Tallulah Falls RR Trail, Tartan Trail

_____

_____

_____

_____

_____

_____

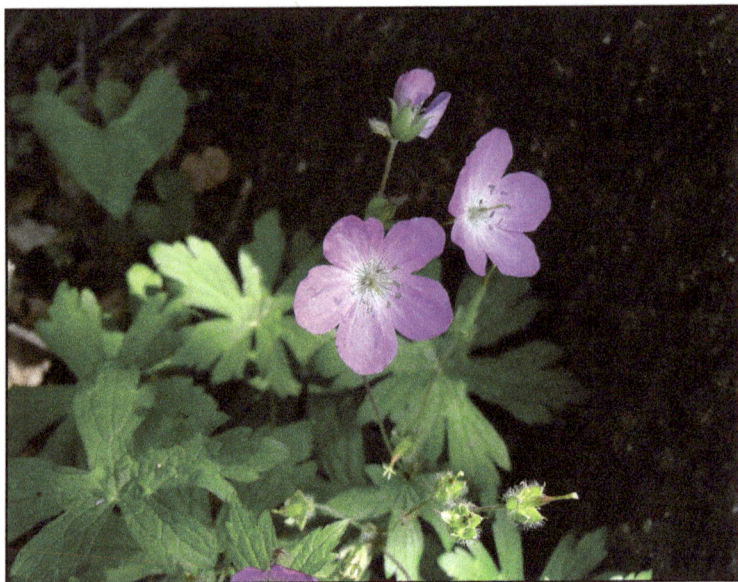

Wild Geranium
Geranium maculatum

Five-petaled rose-pink blooms in spring and early summer rise above deeply lobed leaves of this perennial woodland flower. Like most geraniums, it is recognizable by palmately lobed leaves.

1 to 2' tall with 1 to 1½" flowers and 4 to 5" gray-green leaves.

Geranium family

Tartan Trail, Walasi Trail

Wild Bergamot
Monarda fistulosa

Lavender globes of summer blooms with nectar for butterflies and hummingbirds identify this square-stemmed, aromatic plant with opposite leaves. The leaves are used to make mint tea and it has been used to treat respiratory ailments. Don't confuse it with the red-flowered Bee Balm.

2 to 4' tall with 1" flowers and 2½" long grey-green opposite, lanceolate, coarsely toothed leaves.

Mint family

Old Airport Trail, Tallulah Falls RR Trail, Traders Path.

Spotted Knapweed
Centaurea maculosa

Like lavender stars on their branched stems, these thistle-like flowers bloom all summer. Considered a noxious weed in many western states. The spiny involucre is a prominent feature.

2 to 4' tall with 1" flowers and leaves at the base are 4 to 8" and highly dissected in linear sections.

Composite family

Morris Trace

Joe-Pye-Weed
Eupatorium fistulosum

Huge cluster of pink-purple flowers top this giant late summer blooming plant. Leaves grow in whorls along the single stem.

2 to 6½' tall with 3/8" flowers in a 4 to 5½" cluster and 2½ to 8" whorled leaves on a purple stem.

Composite family

Morris Trace, Old Airport Trail, Tallulah Falls RR Trail

Dense Blazing Star or Gay Feather
Liatris spicata

A spike of reddish-lavender flowers top a sturdy stalk in summer. Prefers low moist ground.

1 to 6' tall with numerous leaves.

Composite family

Tartan Trail

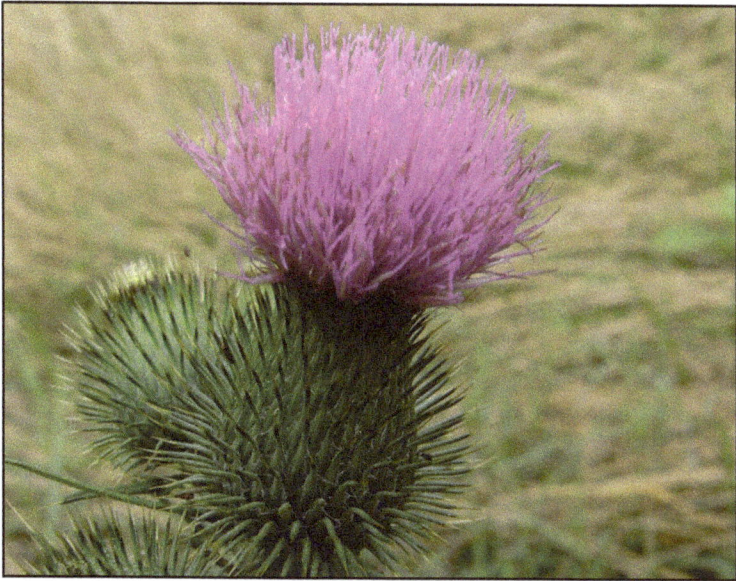

Tall Thistle
Cirsium altissimum

The lavender blooms of thistles attract migrating butterflies. The Cherokees used thistle down for tails of blow gun darts. Look for blooms in summer and fall. Considered a nuisance by farmers for their invasive nature.

4 to 8' tall with 1½ to 2½" flowers borne atop thorny stalks with thorny leaves.

Composite family

Tallulah Falls RR Trail

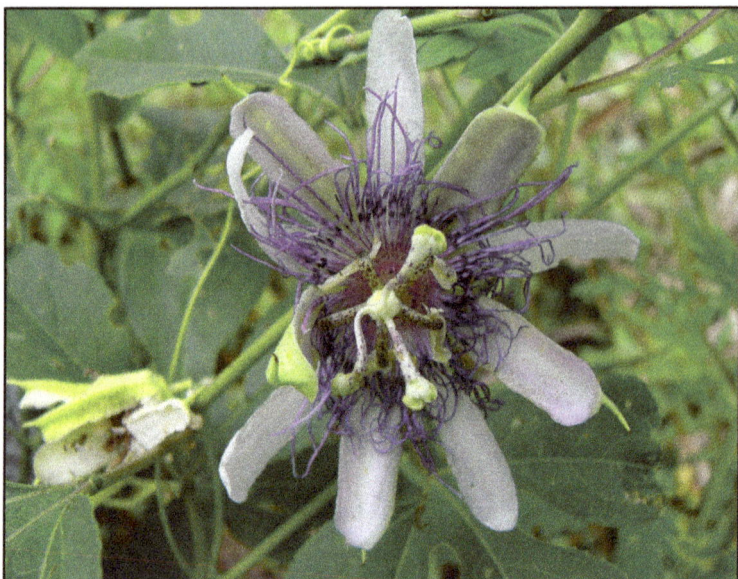

Passionflower or Maypop
Passiflora incarnata

The large, intricate lavender flower of this climbing or trailing vine blooms in summer and produces an edible fruit (maypop). Its name is derived from the flower parts resembling aspects of the Crucifixion. The disciples (minus Peter and Judas) are represented by the 10 petals. The 5 stamens are representative of the 5 wounds; the knobby stigmas, the nails; the crown of thorns, the fringed corona.

6½' long vine with 1 ½ to 2½" flower and 3 to 5" long leaves palmately divided into three section.

Passionflower family

Morris Trace, Old Airport Trail, Tallulah Falls RR Trail

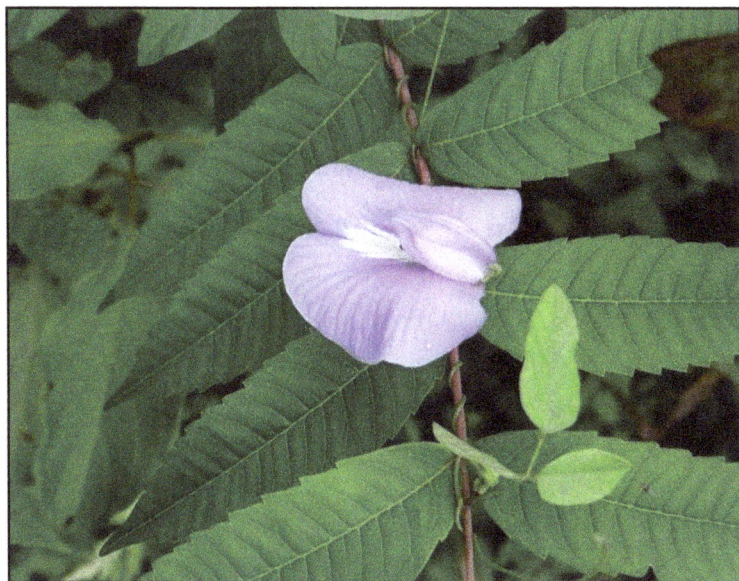

Butterfly Pea
Clitoria mariana

In dry open spaces this trailing vine produces single lavender-blue flowers in summer.

1 to 3" tall with 2" flowers and three ovate leaflets each of which is 1 to 2½" long.

Pea family

Morris Trace, Tartan Trail

_____

_____

_____

_____

_____

_____

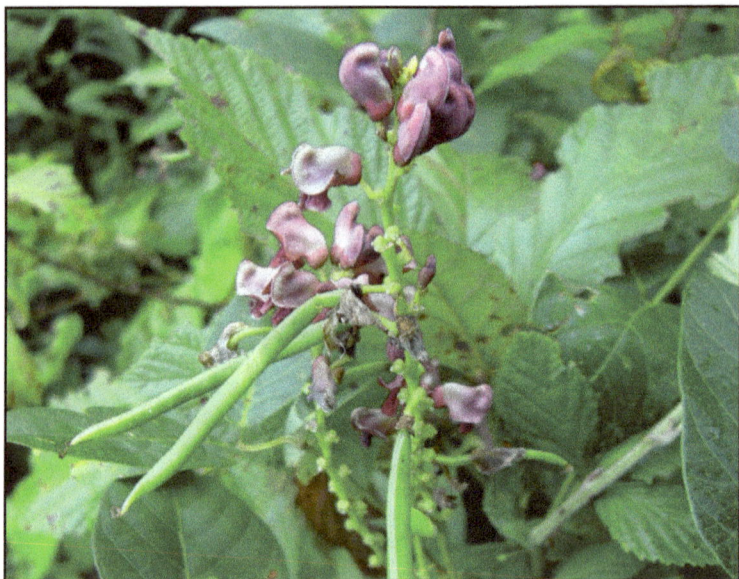

Groundnut
Apios americana

This twining vine with leaves of five to seven leaflets and racemes of purplish flowers has edible tubers as roots - a favorite food of the Cherokees. Tubers can be used in soups or stews or fried like potatoes. The name alludes to its food value. Look for summer blooms.

10' vine with ½" flowers and 4 to 8" leaf.

Pea family

Morris Trace, Old Airport Trail, Tallulah Falls RR Trail, Traders Path

Birdsfoot Violet
Viola pedata

With two violet-colored upper petals, three lavender lower ones, and an orange stamen, this plant can be identified with its spring bloom. It likes dry sunny sites. It takes its name from the shape of its leaf.

4 to 10" tall with 1½" flowers and 1 to 2" long, fan-shaped leaves.

Violet family

Traders Path, Tartan Trail

_____

_____

_____

_____

_____

_____

Purple Dead Nettle
Lamium purpureum

On the upright square stems of the mint family, with drooping greenish-purple leaves, this flower blooms in earliest spring. It enjoys fields and meadows.

3 to 6" tall with ½" flowers and hairy leaves.

Mint family

Old Airport Trail, Tallulah Falls RR Trail, Tartan Trail

_____

_____

_____

_____

_____

_____

Ironweed or Maid of the Meadow
Vernonia noveboracensis

Glowing purple flowers form a cluster above tall purple stems in the late summer. It prefers the damp soil of meadows.

3 to 6' tall with 3/8" flowers and 4 to 8" long finely toothed leaves.

Composite family

Morris Trace, Tallulah Falls RR Trail

Purple-Stemmed Aster
Aster puniceus

This fall-blooming tall bushy blue aster has narrow leaves clasping the stout reddish stem.

2 to 8' tall with 1 to 1½" flower and hairy stem.

Composite family

Morris Trace

Chicory
Cichorium intybus

Blue as an October sky, Chicory is an early riser, nodding off in the afternoon sun. Look for this summer bloomer. The flowers last but one day, showing just a few each day during the blooming season. This European native's root is roasted and ground as a coffee substitute.

1 to 4½' tall with 1½" flowers and 3 to 6" long oblong or lanceolate leaves.

Composite family

Morris Trace

Miami Mist
Phacelia purshii

Recent floods spread the seeds of this lovely blue annual with its fringed petals on many areas of the Greenway. Look for spring blooms.

8 to 16" tall with ½" blooms and closely pressed stem hairs.

Waterleaf family

Old Airport Trail, Tallulah Falls RR Trail, Traders Path, Tartan Trail

Persian Speedwell
Veronica persica

A creeping annual, the four bright blue sepals with darker lines surrounding the pale center, will be found blooming in early spring.

Creeper with ¼" flowers.

Figwort family

Tartan Trail

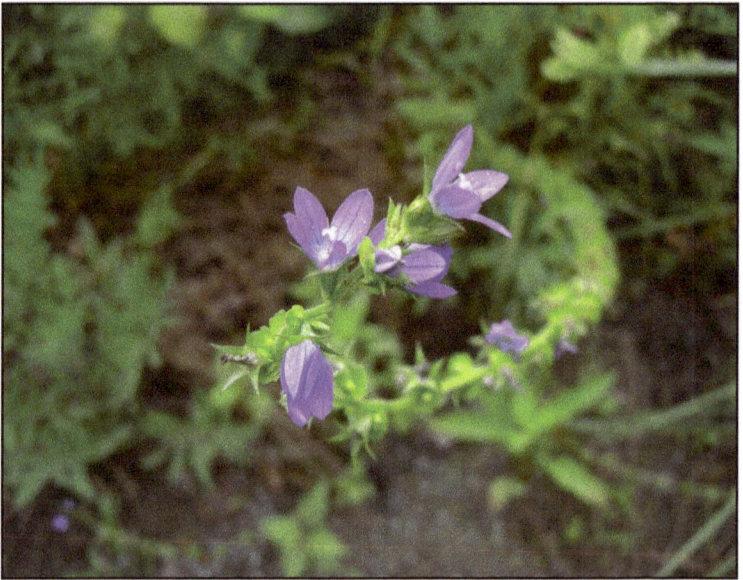

Venus's Looking Glass
Specularia perfoliata

The summer-blooming violet-blue flowers are borne atop an erect stem. They prefer dry woods and fields.

6 to 18" tall with ¾" flowers and ¼ to 1" scallop-toothed, shell-shaped leaves that clasp the stem.

Lobelia family

Morris Trace, Tallulah Falls RR Trail

_____

_____

_____

_____

_____

_____

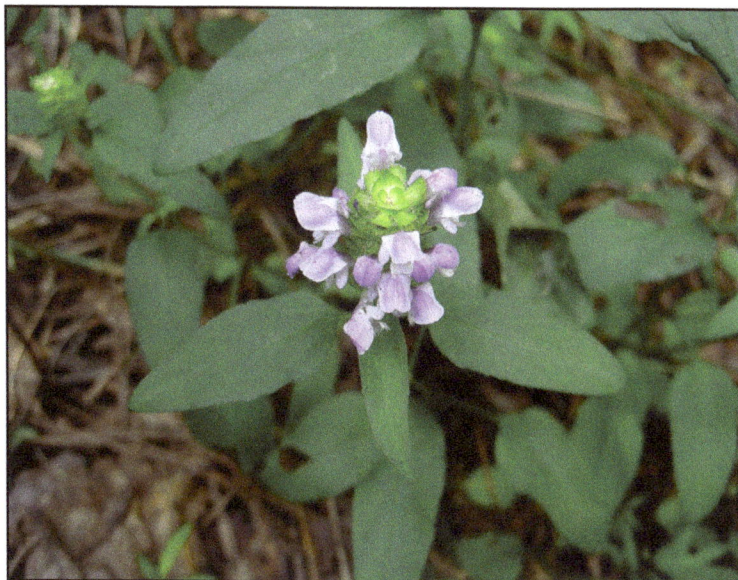

Heal-All
Prunella vulgaris

Atop a square stem, this summer bloomer has blue to purple spikes of flowers. Easily recognized by the many flowered spikes and hairy, overlapping bracts. The name is derived from the plant's use for throat ailments.

6 to 12" tall with ½" flowers and 1 to 3" long lanceolate to oval, opposite leaves.

Mint family

All trail sections

_____

_____

_____

_____

_____

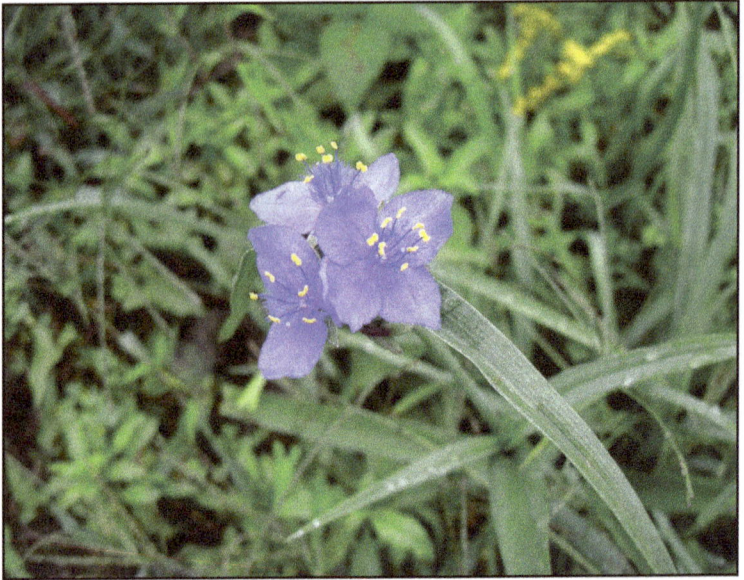

Spiderwort
Tradescantia subaspera

Bright blue three-petalled flowers top these narrow-leaved plants all summer along the Greenway. Each bloom lasts but a day.

8 to 36" tall with 1 to 2" flower and angular leaf arrangement suggesting a squatting spider.

Spiderwort family

All trail sections

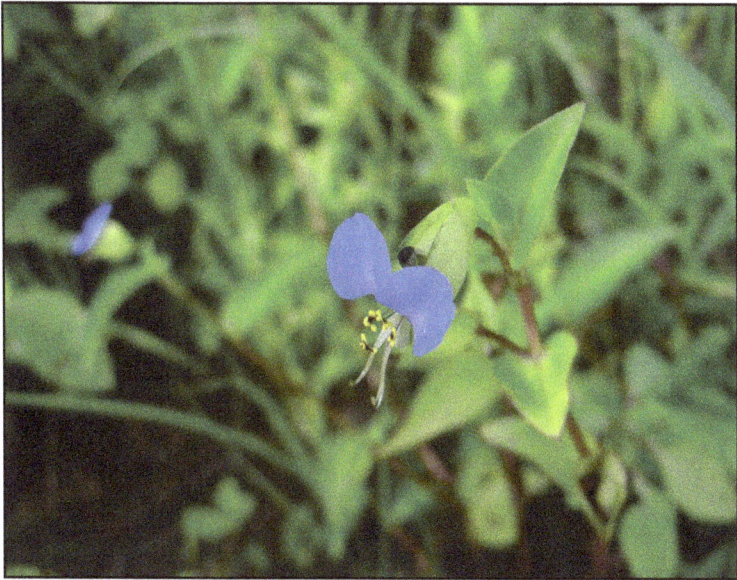

Asiatic Dayflower
Commelina communis

Two blue petals and one white one atop a jointed stem identify this sprawling summer bloomer that was introduced from Asia.

Creeper with ½" flowers protruding from heart-shaped leaflike bract and 3 to 5" fleshy leaves.

Spiderwort family

Old Airport Trail

Hearts-A-Bustin
Euonymus americanus

A green-stemmed shrub found in shady woodlands, in the fall the pink fruits burst to reveal 5 dangling orange seeds.

2 to 6' tall with 2 to 4" stalkless leaves on angled stems.

Staff Tree family

Tallulah Falls RR Trail

_____

_____

_____

_____

_____

_____

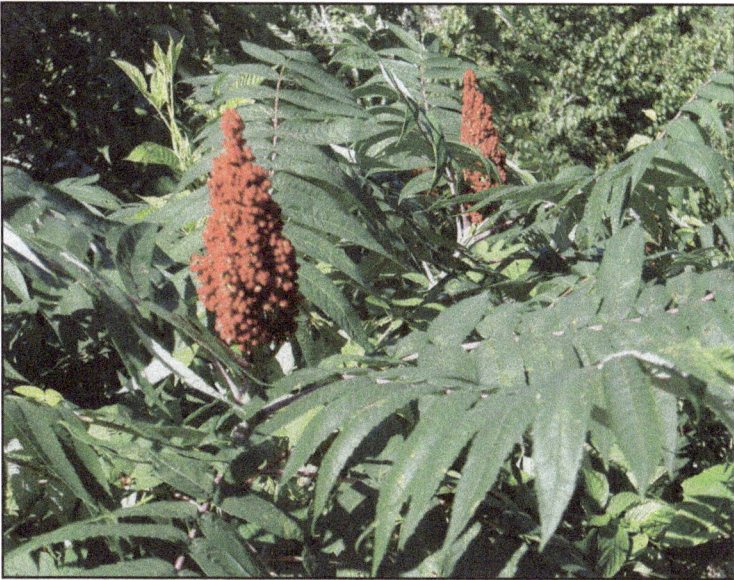

Smooth Sumac
Rhus glabra

A shrub with greenish flowers in terminal clusters in the summer. The fall fruits are in glowing red colors, drying and remaining intact during the winter as wine red berries.

2 to 40' tall with 3 to 12" berry clusters and pinnately divided compound leaves.

Sumac family

All trail sections

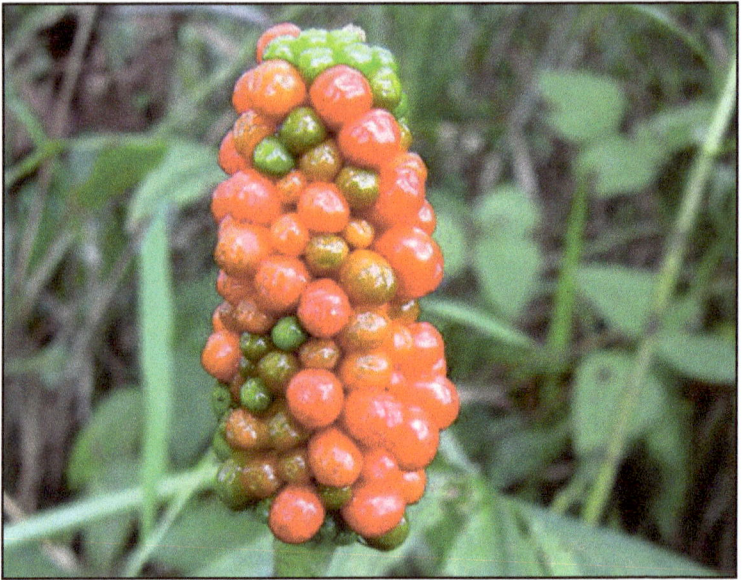

Green Dragon
Arisaema dracontium

Related to Jack-in-the-Pulpit, the solitary leaf of this plant is divided into 5 to 15 segments. The fruit is a dense cluster of scarlet berries. Considered comparatively rare, look for the tiny yellowish-green flowers in late spring.

1 to 3' tall with dull-green pointed leaflets, up to 11" long, coming from a single long shank.

Arum family

Old Airport Trail, Tallulah Falls RR Trail

Pokeweed
Phytolacca americana

The racemes of small white flowers and glossy black berries appear together from spring through fall on this branching plant. Natives use the tender shoots of the plant in the spring for "poke salat", after boiling through several waters to remove poison. The berries are poisonous as well.

3 to 10' tall with ¼" flowers and berries and elliptical-lanceolate leaves.

Pokeweed family

All trail sections

Elderberry
Sambucus canadensis

The purplish black fruit of this large shrub are used for making pies, jellies, and wine and are an important source of food for birds.

3 to 12' tall with white clusters of blooms can be seen in June and July.

Honeysuckle family

Morris Trace, Old Airport Trail, Tallulah Falls RR Trail, Traders Path

Chinese Privet
Ligustrum sinense

The berries of this nonnative shrub or small tree mature in the fall. It is covered in white cluster of fragrant flowers in the spring. The berries are considered poisonous but the birds love them.

20' tall with ½" deciduous, opposite leaves in two rows.

Olive family

All trail sections

_____

_____

_____

_____

_____

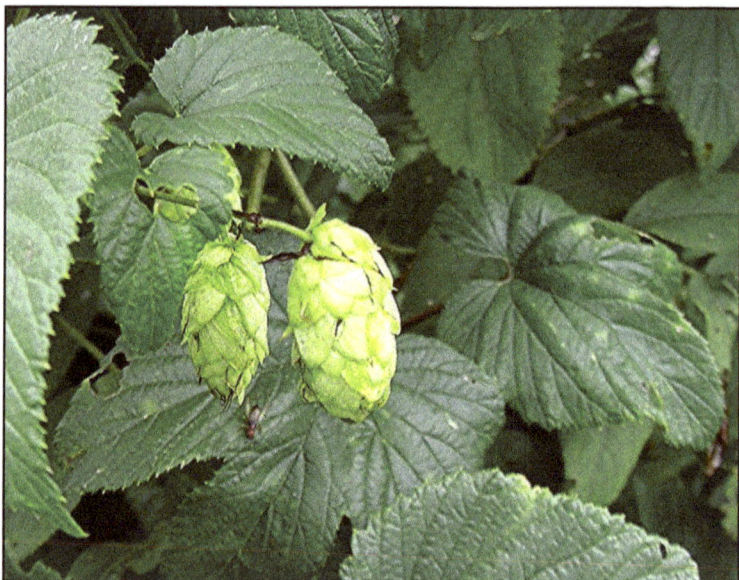

Common Hop
Humulus lupulus

The fruit of this twining vine is a cone of overlapping bracts. It climbs the rivercane and brambles.

Hemp family

Old Airport Trail

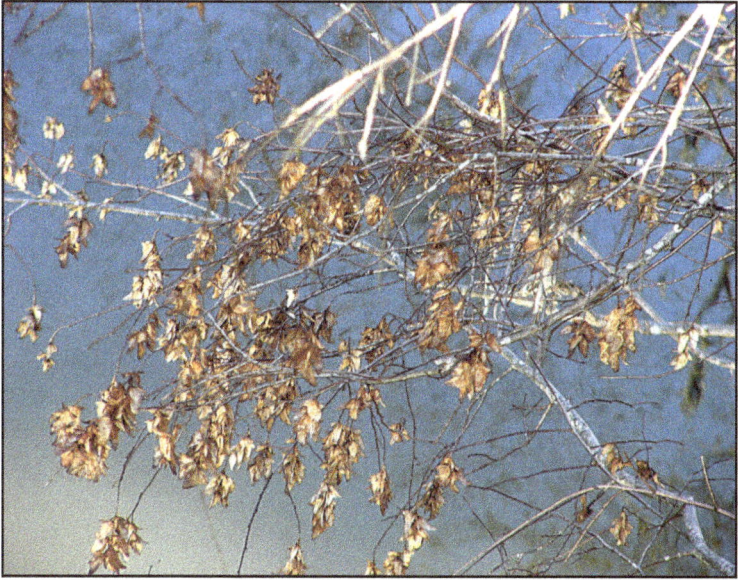

Ironwood
Carpinus caroliniana

A shrubby tree with smooth gray angled trunk. Fruits are tiny nutlets attached to three pointed leafy bracts.

20 to 50' tall with 2 to 5" ovate or sharply elliptical leaves of a dull yellow-green.

Birch family

Tallulah Falls RR Trail, Traders Path

_____

_____

_____

_____

_____

_____

Sycamore
Platanus occidentalis

A common sight along the Greenway, the sycamore's fruit is a 1" brown ball, maturing in the fall and often hanging from the tree during the winter.

This large tree is identified by its smooth, light-colored bark that peels in large flakes, creating a mottled appearance, and large maple-like leaves. It enjoys growing on banks, shading the river and the Greenway.

Sycamore family

All trail sections

Tag Alder
Alnus serrulata

A large spreading shrub commonly found near water. The drooping male catkins appear in winter, and in spring produce a golden pollen. It enjoys growing along wet water edges in thickets that provide cover for deer and seeds for birds.

10 to 20' tall with 1 to 5" elliptical or ovate leaves and a smooth gray bark.

Birch family

All trail sections

_____

_____

_____

_____

_____

Catalpa
Catalpa bignonioides

The "Indian Bean" grows on a tree that may reach 50' tall. The fruit is 6 to 12" long and will remain on the tree through most of the winter. The heart-shaped leaves in whorled clusters of three are dull green and pale with soft hairs below.

Bigonia family

All trail sections

_____

_____

_____

_____

_____

_____

Black Locust
Robinia pseudoacacia

A spiny tree with fragrant white clusters of bloom in spring, brown bean-like seed pods remain attached into winter.

40 to 80' tall with 2 to 4" seed pods. The bark is light grey and deeply furrowed. Leaves are 6 to 12" long and pinnately compounded. Paired thorns protrude at leaf bases.

Pea family

All trail sections

_____

_____

_____

_____

_____

Silverbell
Halesia carolina

In April and May the branches of this tree are hung with white bell-shaped blooms. Look for the seed pods in the winter. See flower on page 21.

Storax family

All trail sections

_____

_____

_____

_____

_____

_____

_____

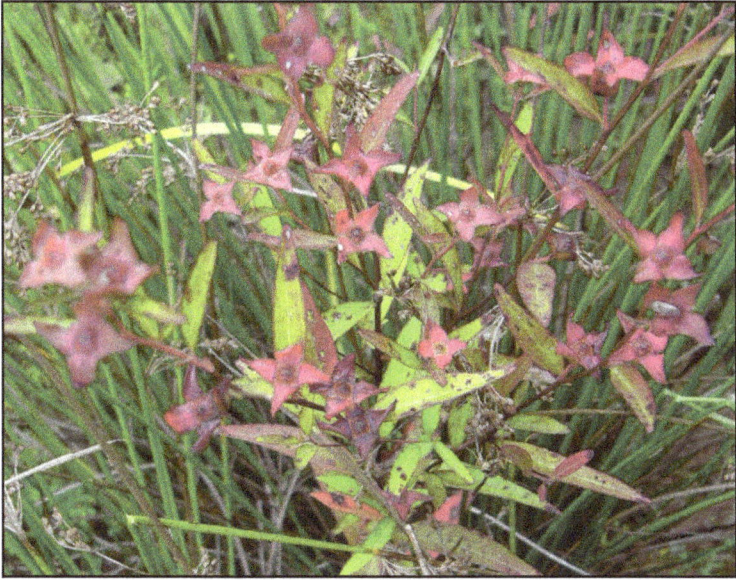

Seedbox
Ludwigia alternifolia

The four-winged boxlike seed capsules growing in leaf axils become bright pink in the fall. See page 32 for the plant in bloom.

Evening Primrose family

Morris Trace, Old Airport Trail, Tallulah Falls RR Trail

_____

_____

_____

_____

_____

_____

_____

Index

Index

Friends Of the Greenway

573 East Main Street
Franklin, NC, 28734
828.369.8488
www.LittleTennessee.org

www.ingramcontent.com/pod-product-compliance
Lightning Source LLC
Chambersburg PA
CBHW050843270326
41930CB00019B/3449